# ENGLAND
## *of One Hundred Years Ago*
# PHOTOGRAPH COLLECTION

# SOUTH WILTSHIRE

## SELECTED BY DAVID BUXTON

ALAN SUTTON

First published in the United Kingdom in 1992
by Alan Sutton Publishing Limited
Phoenix Mill, Stroud, Gloucestershire

First published in the United States of America
by Alan Sutton Publishing Incorporated
83 Washington Avenue, Dover, New Hampshire

Copyright © Alan Sutton Publishing Limited, 1992

British Library and Library of Congress
Cataloguing in Publication Data applied for

ISBN 0-7509-0305-8

Typesetting and origination by
Alan Sutton Publishing Limited
Graphics and Design Department.
Printed in Great Britain by
Bath Colour Books.

Some blemishes have been removed by extreme enlargement of the image to individual pixel
level, with careful computer graphics surgery to mend scratches, foxing, or other damage to the
photographic image.

# ENGLAND
## *of One Hundred Years Ago*
# VOLUME SEVEN

# South Wiltshire

The photograph collection of England of One Hundred Years Ago is an attempt to find and produce some of the best images in existence from late Victorian times up to the onset of the First World War. The country has been split into the traditional counties and this volume, numbered 7, represents South Wiltshire.

The criteria for selection are quality and clarity in the image together with subject interest. An attempt has been made to ensure a reasonable geographical balance within the area covered, but it has to be admitted that some areas were much more photographed than others.

The printed images are intended to be used for framing, although some people may wish to buy additional separate prints for framing by using the order form at the back of the book, and to keep this book intact. If the order form becomes separated from the book please write to the Phoenix Mill address advising the volume number and plate number you require.

The reproductions in this book are obtained by digital scanning and computer enhancement. Some blemishes have been removed by extreme enlargement of the image to individual pixel level, with careful computer graphics surgery to mend scratches, foxing, or other damage to the photographic image. The pictures on the facing page show a scratch, enlarged and repaired. Some damage, or blemishes in an otherwise interesting photograph are beyond

reasonable repair, and have been left.

The monochrome image is then further enhanced by being artificially separated and printed in a four colour process with a sepia bias. The result is a high quality image with visual depth. The finished printed image is then protected by a careful application of matt varnish to reduce fading and to add protection. The paper is a super-calendared, acid free, matt art of 170 grammes weight per square metre.

The contents of the photographs remain totally genuine and the enhancement and surgery are used only to mend damage and not to create artificial images!

South Wiltshire of one hundred years ago was, as it is largely today, an agricultural area. On the lonely expanses of the Plain, thousands of sheep grazed, overlooked by patient shepherds, disturbed only occasionally by the sounds of soldiers in training. The army had already begun to see the Plain as a useful excercise area. The great monument of Stonehenge and the magnificent Cathedral in Salisbury both attracted visitors to the area but most people in the county led parochial lives, unaffected by happenings taking place outside their own village. The pictures included in this small selection from South Wiltshire could not provide a comprehensive view but they do present a fascinating cameo of life in the county of that time.

# Contents

Acknowledgements.

I should like to thank the following people and organizations for allowing me to use their photographs: Bourne Valley History Group, Mr Tony Lyons, Mr A. Moulding, Salisbury and South Wilts Museum, Warminster Museum, Wiltshire Library and Museum Service.

Plate 1. ST ANN'S GATE
Close gateway, Salisbury, *c.* 1890

Plate 2. SHEPHERD AND HIS SHEEP
Shepherd on Salisbury Plain near Stonehenge, *c.* 1895

Plate 3. VILLAGE CHILDREN
The churchyard at Fisherton de la Mere, *c.* 1895

Plate 4. FAMILY OF THE CLOSE
A Victorian family in the Cathedral Close, Salisbury, *c.* 1900

Plate 5. COUNTRY BREWERY
The Castle Street Brewery, Salisbury, *c.* 1895

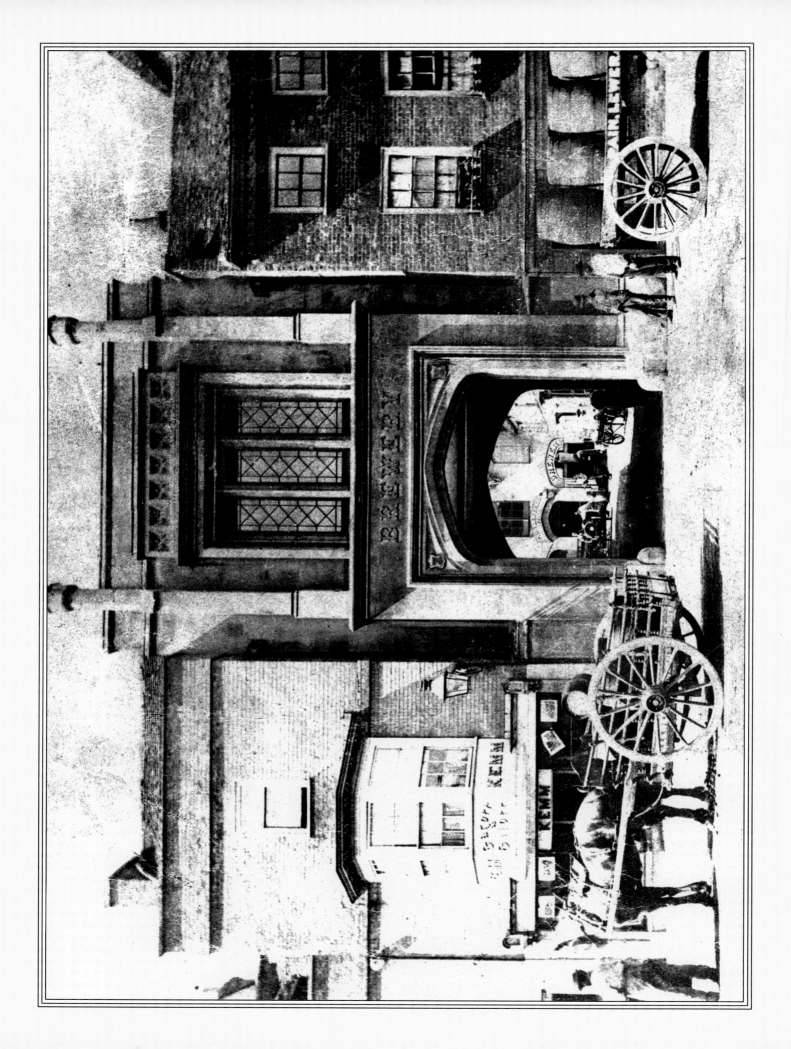

Plate 8. HEART OF THE VILLAGE
Alderbury Post Office, *c.* 1895

Plate 7. COTTAGE ECONOMY
A Wiltshire cottager, Fisherton de la Mere, *c*. 1895

Plate 6. BAILIFF'S COTTAGE

Cottage by the River Wylye, Fisherton de la Mere, *c.* 1895

Plate 9. GOING TO MARKET
Market day in Warminster, *c.* 1900

Plate 10. A WILTSHIRE MEADOW
A view of Warminster from the South, *c.* 1900

Plate 11. GROVELY! GROVELY! GROVELY!
Oak-apple Day ceremony in Great Wishford, 1906

Plate 12. THE CLOSE GATE
Salisbury North Gate, High Street, *c.* 1895

Plate 13. SALISBURY SPIRE
Salisbury Cathedral from across the river, *c.* 1895

Plate 14. THE POULTRY CROSS
Butcher Row, Salisbury, *c.* 1900

Plate 15. STONES ON THE PLAIN

Stonehenge on Salisbury Plain, 1887

Plate 16. THE ANCIENT CROSS
The Poultry Cross and Minster Street, Salisbury, 1887

Plate 17. THE OLD ROSE AND CROWN
Harnham village, Salisbury, 1906

Plate 18. SPLENDOUR IN STONE
Salisbury Cathedral from the North West, 1887

Plate 19. A WILTSHIRE THATCH
Waterstreet Farm, Watery Lane, Donhead, *c.* 1900

Plate 20. WE THREE ON THE FARM
The farmer's children, Waterstreet Farm, Watery Lane, Donhead, *c.* 1900

Plate 21. VILLAGE CHURCH
Interior of St Mary's Church, Winterbourne Gunner, 1898

Plate 22. SARSEN STONES
Stonehenge, Salisbury Plain, *c.* 1900

Plate 23. RAISING A GIANT
Re-erecting one of the fallen sarsen stones, Stonehenge, *c.* 1900

Plate 24. MR AND MRS BLAKE AND THEIR SERVANTS
Mr and Mrs Blake and their servants at The Elms, Winterbourne Gunner,
1895

Plate 25. A COUNTRY GARDEN
The garden of The Elms, Winterbourne Gunner, *c.* 1895

Plate 26. MEET BY THE BRIDGE
The post office and bridge, Newton Toney, Salisbury, *c.* 1905

Plate 27. THE WATER CARRIER
White Bridge, Winterbourne Gunner, *c.* 1905

Plate 28. CYCLE CLUB DAY OUT
Devizes Cycle Club at Stonehenge, 1895